D1067330

SAFEGUARDING WATER AND FOOD SUPPLIES

rosen publishing's
rosen
central®

Published in 2013 by The Rosen Publishing Group, Inc.
29 East 21st Street, New York, NY 10010

First Edition

Library of Congress Cataloging-in-Publication Data
Craig, Joe.
Safeguarding water and food supplies/Joe Craig.—1st ed.
    p. cm.—(Science to the rescue: adapting to climate change)
Includes bibliographical references and index.
ISBN 978-1-4488-6851-3 (library binding)
1. Water-supply–Security measures–United States. 2. Food supply–Security measures–United States. 3. Water conservation–United States. 4. Food conservation–United States. I. Title.
TD223.C726 2013
363.8'20973–dc23
                                                                2011052044

Manufactured in the United States of America

CPSIA Compliance Information: Batch #S12YA: For further information, contact Rosen Publishing, New York, New York, at 1-800-237-9932.

CONtents

INTROduction

Malnutrition caused by hunger is the number one risk to human health worldwide—greater than malaria, AIDS, and tuberculosis combined. Currently, there are 925 million undernourished people in the world. In 2011, the United Nations declared a famine in Somalia. Regional conflict, poverty, and East Africa's worst drought in half a century stalled food production there. Worldwide, 70 percent of all freshwater is used for agriculture. During a drought, people can't get access to water, and food production suffers. Millions in Somalia were at risk for death caused by drought- and famine-related starvation, thirst, and disease. Somalis fled their homes in search of food. Tens of thousands died, half of them children.

One billion people in the world do not have access to safe water. Half of the world's hospitalizations are prompted by water-related diseases. Almost one-and-a-half million children die every year from these illnesses. This is largely because of poverty and social conflict, but droughts make the situation exponentially worse.

Food production and water supplies are inseparably linked to the climate, and Earth's climate is changing as a

result of global warming. Droughts used to occur every six to eight years in East Africa, but now they occur every one or two years. The average temperature in the United States has risen 2 degrees Fahrenheit (1.1 degrees Celsius) in the past fifty years, and it continues to rise. The climate changes that are coming and already underway are threatening our food and water supplies. Higher temperatures and unpredictable

Children collect dirty drinking water from a broken pipe. One billion people in the world don't have access to clean and safe water.

rainfall will cause more drought and famine. Global stability and millions of lives are at stake. And we're the ones who are responsible.

Human activities like industry, agriculture, transportation, and deforestation are causing global warming and climate change. Climate change is any large, measurable change in climate, such as temperature (for example, global warming), rainfall, or wind, lasting for a long period of time (decades or more). Climate change is such an enormous, complex, and daunting problem that it can seem insurmountable to the average person. How can humans possibly reverse the profound climate changes that they have set in motion ever since the beginning of the Industrial Age?

Thankfully, the brightest minds are working on ways to slow the effects of climate change, limit its impact, and allow humans to adapt to the unavoidable changes that are on the way. For example, international cooperation has made it possible to begin saving different seed types in the Svalbard Global Seed Vault in Svalbard, Norway. The seed vault is a final safety net against global famine and crop, plant, and tree extinctions. The vault holds samples of more than 526,000 unique crop varieties. Engineers are also perfecting methods to conserve water, such as special water tanks that harvest rainfall. And there are many promising innovations just around the corner, like artificial trees that absorb carbon from the atmosphere.

Without question, we have an enormous challenge ahead of us. Climate change may turn out to be mostly irreversible. There are no easy solutions. But if we're focused, passionate, and united, we can adapt to, overcome, and blunt the worst effects of climate change. As those most responsible for climate change, we humans have no choice but to try.

CHAPTER one

Human Activity and Threatened Food and Water Supplies

Earth's climate is definitely changing. Average global surface temperatures have risen since 1880, and they continue to increase at an accelerating rate. In 2003, Europe experienced its hottest summer in almost five hundred years. The heat wave killed more than forty thousand people. In the United States, heat waves kill more people every year than tornadoes, hurricanes, earthquakes, or any other natural disaster combined. In the future, heat waves will occur more often and last longer. The oceans are getting hotter, too, as they absorb the sun's heat from the air. The top 2,300 feet (701 meters) of ocean water have warmed 0.302°F (0.167°C) since 1969. Ice sheets are melting, glaciers are retreating, sea levels are rising, oceans are becoming more acidic, and extreme weather events are occurring more often, all because of rising temperatures.

Climate change is putting our food and water supplies in danger. If we don't quickly correct our way of life, we may irreparably damage the planet and our future. It's a hot topic today, as it should be. But why is climate change such an important issue? How long has it been going on, and how did it begin?

THE GREENHOUSE EFFECT

The greenhouse effect is the process in which infrared radiation—invisible frequencies of the sun's light and heat—is absorbed by certain gases in the atmosphere, called greenhouse gases (GHGs), and reradiated down to Earth. The process works like a greenhouse, which is built to trap the sun's heat. In short, greenhouse gases warm the planet by trapping heat from the sun.

Greenhouse gases are extremely important. Without them, Earth would be an uninhabitable, frozen wasteland. Global surface temperatures would average 0°F (-18°C). Conversely, with too high a quantity of greenhouse gases, Earth would be like Venus, where the average surface temperature is 860°F (460°C). Until relatively recently, Earth's atmosphere contained the ideal level of greenhouse gases necessary for life.

The main greenhouse gases in Earth's atmosphere are water vapor (H_2O), carbon dioxide (CO_2), methane (CH_4), nitrous oxide (N_2O), and ozone (O_3). Other gases, such as chlorofluorocarbons (CFCs), are also present, but in small percentages. As previously stated, some greenhouse gases occur naturally. Carbon dioxide is produced when humans

The sun sends infrared radiation to Earth. Greenhouse gases in the atmosphere trap a certain amount of that radiation and reflect it back to Earth. This process, known as the greenhouse effect, heats Earth's surface and makes the planet less habitable.

and animals exhale. It is then absorbed by plants, which require it for photosynthesis and then emit oxygen as a waste product of the process. Volcanic eruptions can also release carbon dioxide from rocks deep inside the planet. Methane is created through many different natural processes in low-oxygen environments, like swamps, rivers, and even the digestive tracts of animals. Water vapor is simply the gas phase of water.

Certain human activities create greenhouse gases, too. Landfills and grazing livestock, such as cows, emit methane. Nitrous oxide enters waterways and the atmosphere from fertilizers. Deforestation prevents carbon dioxide absorption by trees, resulting in a buildup of the gas in the atmosphere. Chlorofluorocarbons are used in refrigeration and in aerosol cans, and are released into the air with each spray or following leaks. However, humanity's largest source of greenhouse gas emissions, by far, is the carbon dioxide emitted when fossil fuels—like oil, coal, and natural gas—are burned.

HUMAN ACTIVITY AND GLOBAL WARMING

We burn fossil fuels like oil, natural gas, and coal for energy. We use that energy for transportation; to power industry; and to provide heat, air-conditioning, and electricity to homes and businesses. Fossil fuels are formed from organisms that lived hundreds of millions of years ago, even before the first dinosaurs. When those organisms (plants, animals, and bacteria) died, they were buried under layers of rock, soil, and water. They then decomposed into simpler forms of organic material, becoming fossil fuels.

When they are burned, fossil fuels release lots of energy, yet they also release lots of carbon dioxide. That CO_2 enters the atmosphere and contributes to global warming more than any other greenhouse gas. For this reason, scientists talk about all greenhouse gases based on their equivalent in carbon dioxide.

Humans have been burning fossil fuels for thousands of years, but not in significant amounts until the Industrial Revolution. This was a period of enormous technological advances in agriculture, mining, transportation, textiles, manufacturing, and infrastructure that affected almost every aspect of daily life. Steam power paved the way. Steam engines, used in machinery and transportation, burned coal to boil water and create the steam that powered their mechanisms. This marked the beginning of humanity's ever-growing dependence on fossil fuel. Since the start of the Industrial Revolution, five hundred billion tons of CO_2 have been emitted into the atmosphere, where it lingers for a very long time, absorbing more and more heat.

Cars burn gasoline—a fossil fuel—and release CO_2 into the atmosphere. CO_2 from fossil fuels contributes to global warming more than any other greenhouse gas does.

THE GREEN REVOLUTION

Starting in the 1940s, many countries invested in scientific research to improve farming and food production. Scientists selected, bred, and genetically enhanced crops and livestock to increase their growth rate and their resistance to certain diseases. They also developed pesticides, synthetic fertilizers, and irrigation methods to improve growing conditions.

The so-called Green Revolution was the period from the 1960s to 1990s when these new farming practices increased food production in developing countries like India and Mexico. During this time, yields, or the amount produced, of wheat, rice, and corn more than doubled. The revolution prevented famine and mass starvation around the world.

But there have been many unintended consequences. For example, the widespread use of chemicals (like pesticides) has polluted the environment. Agricultural biodiversity, or the variety of crop and livestock species, has decreased because farmers have abandoned their local species for the genetically enhanced high-yield ones. Water supplies have been polluted and overused. Most important, people still go hungry every day.

Today, new problems like climate change threaten food production and water supplies. Just like during the Green Revolution, we'll have to use our brains to tackle these challenges and feed the world's growing population.

Yet climate change is not a new or recent phenomenon. Earth's climate has changed several times throughout history, even before the Industrial Revolution and the sharp increase in carbon emissions into the atmosphere. According to the National Aeronautic and Space Administration (NASA), there have been seven cycles of climate change in the last 650,000 years. There are many possible natural causes for these cycles, like changes in the sun's intensity, variations in Earth's orbit, and plate tectonics.

If Earth's climate has always been changing, since even before the Industrial Revolution, how do we know humans are to blame for this most recent period of climate change? We know human activity is driving the current warming of the planet and resulting climate change because Earth is getting warmer far more quickly than at any other time in the past 1,300 years. In fact, the warmest years on record have all occurred since 1998. In the last century, the global sea level rose 6.7 inches (17 centimeters) due to melting glaciers and ice caps, and the rate of sea level increase in the last decade is almost double that of the last century.

At the same time, we're burning more fossil fuels than ever. Since 1990, yearly emissions have increased by 20 percent, or six billion metric tons of carbon dioxide equivalent. There is a greater abundance of carbon dioxide in the atmosphere now than at any point in the past eight hundred thousand years. Methane is at its highest level in four hundred thousand years. The climate change that is now occurring is entirely consistent with the way humans are treating the environment. It is the direct consequence of our modern, industrialized lifestyles.

HOW FOOD PRODUCTION WILL BE AFFECTED

Climate change will seriously impact agriculture. Crops need specific weather conditions in order to survive. In the future, global temperatures, precipitation, pollution, and severe weather events will determine whether or not we'll be able to produce enough food for the growing population.

Different regions will be affected differently. For example, the northern regions of the United States will become wetter, while southern areas, especially the Southwest, will become even drier than they already are. Certain areas will get too hot and dry for crop production and will be prone to more frequent and devastating wildfires.

Agriculture all around the world will be disrupted by severe weather events, like droughts, heat waves, and floods. These severe weather events will be more frequent and intense than ever before.

HOW FRESHWATER WILL BE AFFECTED

Water is all around us. It's in the beverages we drink and the food we eat. Water is used to manufacture goods, irrigate crops, cool power plants, and create electricity. It's in the sky and it's underground. It's even inside of the human body. Water is so present that we take it for granted. It may seem like we have plenty, but of all the water on Earth, 97 percent is undrinkable saltwater. Less than 3 percent is freshwater, and two-thirds of that is frozen in glaciers and ice caps. In many parts of the world, water is scarce. Climate change is

A crowd watches the swollen Whetstone Brook barrel through Brattleboro, Vermont. The remnants of Hurricane Irene brought torrential rain, flooding Brattleboro and other areas throughout New England. In the future, floods may occur more frequently in the northeastern part of the United States.

aggravating the issue, threatening our access to the clean water we need.

Hotter temperatures accelerate ice melt and water evaporation into the atmosphere. That extra water vapor is a greenhouse gas, and it warms Earth even more. Water vapor turns into precipitation (rain, snow, or hail), so more atmospheric water vapor means more precipitation. Over the past fifty years, rainfall has increased in the Northeast and Midwest of the United States. Storms are shifting northward, so rainfall in the Southeast and West has actually decreased. All around the world, precipitation has changed in frequency, location, and intensity. In the future, floods and droughts will be more frequent and severe. We'll see too little water in some places and too much in others.

Some places could even see both floods and droughts at different times of the year.

Water quality is very sensitive to fluctuations in temperature and rainfall. Increased rainfall can actually increase water pollution by washing more pollutants from land surfaces into waterways. Floods can overload wastewater systems. Rising oceans may intrude on groundwater supplies (water pumped up from underground) and make them too salty to drink or use. Contaminated water supplies mean there is less to drink and use for crops.

Drought will likely affect many of the world's major cities. In fact, there have already been water shortages in Barcelona, Spain, and Melbourne, Australia, affecting their combined population of nine million people. Phoenix, Arizona; Los Angeles, California; and Las Vegas, Nevada, could soon find themselves in similar situations. Presently, there is as much water on Earth as there ever was and ever will be. Yet the world's population grows every day. Water will be a key issue in global politics in the future. Conflict, some of it violent, will grow over dwindling supplies.

The future sounds grim, but there is hope. Scientists believe that the effects of climate change can be minimized or successfully adapted to. Human ingenuity and adaptability have overcome impossible problems in the past. If we're serious, focused, passionate, and united, we can overcome climate change and protect our food and water supplies. Humans are responsible for the problem, so we are also responsible for finding a solution. We must both protect the planet and safeguard the lives of future generations.

CHAPTER two

Changing Climate, Changing Practices

Experts are researching climate change in order to propose potential solutions. Scientists and engineers generally agree that we should focus our efforts on both mitigation—lessening climate change's force—and adaptation. Mitigation involves limiting the effects of climate change. We can do that by conserving energy and water, for example. If certain effects of climate change aren't preventable, as some scientists believe, we'll have to adapt. We will be forced to change our way of life through behavior or technology to suit the changing climate.

Climate change is an extremely complicated subject. It's not as simple as reducing greenhouse gas emissions. In fact, experts are still discovering the causes of climate change and how it will affect our water and food supplies in the future.

FOOD BIODIVERSITY

Most of us have heard something about plant and animal extinctions in rain forests around the world. Very few of us, however, know anything about food variety extinction. Believe it or not, there used to be 285 different types of cucumbers on Earth. Now there are sixteen. That's because over the course of human history, farmers created food biodiversity by selectively breeding crops and livestock that were particularly suited to their local climate. But after the Green Revolution (see page 12), farmers favored a small number of high-yield, genetically enhanced species. Today, farmers all around the world rely on the same few breeds of crops and livestock. The desire for increased production has doomed local varieties to extinction, decreasing biodiversity. In the United States, about 90 percent of our fruit and vegetable varieties have already gone extinct.

That's a problem. The crops and livestock that we rely upon were genetically enhanced for one thing: greater yields. To survive in as many different climates as possible, the crops require expensive pesticides and fertilizers, while the livestock must consume special feed. High-yield varieties are weaker than their local counterparts. They may lack the proper genes and immunities to survive climate change or disease.

Currently, *Puccinia graminis*, a fungus also called stem rust, is spreading around the world. Most farmers rely on the same few species of genetically enhanced wheat. According to *National Geographic*, "[R]oughly 90 percent of the world's wheat is defenseless against Ug99" (the name of this particular strain of fungus). Stem rust could leave one billion people starving in Africa and Asia alone. If it continues to spread, it could reach North America, too.

Climate change and disease will continue to threaten our food sources. Food biodiversity is a safety net.

Most people don't realize how many different types of tomatoes there are. That's because most farmers today rely on the same few breeds of genetically engineered, high-yield crops. The tomatoes shown here are rare heirloom varieties grown by a farmer in Pennington, New Jersey.

For example, there may be a local species of wheat that's immune to stem rust. Hopefully, we haven't let that species go extinct.

RETHINKING FARMING PRACTICES

Just as climate change affects agriculture, agriculture affects climate change. Agriculture contributes to climate change by releasing CO_2 through deforestation, methane from rice cultivation and manure, and nitrous oxide from fertilizers. It also pollutes water supplies.

We can't simply write off conventional, high-yield farming practices, however. They have degraded the environment and contributed to climate change, but they've also saved billions of people from starving. Alternative farming practices may pollute less, but they also typically produce smaller yields. In the future, we'll need to increase food production by 70 to 100 percent, protect food supplies from climate change, and limit the agricultural industry's impact on the environment. But is it possible to grow more food for more people without producing negative environmental consequences?

Regardless of the answer to that question, we have to make changes to the way we raise and produce food. In spite of the Green Revolution, 925 million people are currently undernourished worldwide. That's a seventh of the world's population. Sustainability is key. As the population grows and the planet gets warmer, our limited resources will be stretched even further. We need more efficient farms that use fewer resources. The United Nations suggests supporting small-scale farms in developing countries. These farms can increase sustainable food production and decrease rural poverty.

There are no simple solutions for ending world hunger. It is clear that we need to minimize our impact on the environment. Climate change will cause drought and famine. We need as much food as possible, but if we continue to pollute for short-term gain, we'll only hurt our chances of future survival.

In Mogadishu, Somalia, a mother holds her malnourished baby. One-seventh of the world's population is undernourished.

GRAPPLING WITH NONPOINT WATER POLLUTION

In 2010, an explosion on the British Petroleum *Deepwater Horizon* oil-drilling rig killed eleven men and exposed an oil gusher on the ocean floor. About 170 million gallons (643,520,040 liters) of oil leaked into the Gulf of Mexico over the course of three months. Over eight thousand birds, sea turtles, and mammals were found injured or dead. But all that pollution is nothing compared to nonpoint water pollution.

When we think of water pollution, most of us imagine major disasters or factories spewing waste into rivers. Actually, most water pollution is caused by nonpoint sources, or sources that pollute indirectly. Runoff, for example, occurs when excess water, like rainfall, flows over the land. That runoff carries pollutants on the ground, like oil slicks, pesticides, or fertilizers, into waterways. Agricultural runoff has become the biggest source of water pollution in America. In the United

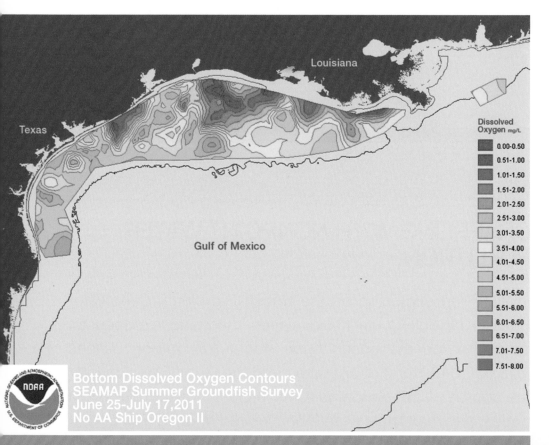

Louisiana

Texas

Dissolved
Oxygen mg/L

0.00-0.50
0.51-1.00
1.01-1.50
1.51-2.00
2.01-2.50
2.51-3.00
3.01-3.50
3.51-4.00
4.01-4.50
4.51-5.00
5.01-5.50
5.51-6.00
6.01-6.50
6.51-7.00
7.01-7.50
7.51-8.00

Gulf of Mexico

nOAA

Bottom Dissolved Oxygen Contours
SEAMAP Summer Groundfish Survey
June 25-July 17, 2011
No AA Ship Oregon II

The Mississippi River deposits agricultural runoff into the Gulf of Mexico, creating a dead zone the size of New Jersey. The red spots highlight the areas of greatest oxygen depletion.

States, livestock produce one billion tons of manure each year. Harmful bacteria, viruses, and parasites from manure seep into underground waterways and are washed into rivers by runoff. Almost twenty million Americans are sickened every year from drinking contaminated water.

Manure also contains phosphorous and nitrogen from cattle feed and supplements, which chemically alter and damage aquatic ecosystems. When fertilizer leaks into waterways, it can actually fertilize algae. The algae bloom, die, and suck the oxygen out of the water. These oxygen-deprived areas are known as dead zones because no organism can survive within them. Dead zones have already appeared at the mouths of most major rivers. Where the Mississippi River empties into the Gulf of Mexico, there's a dead zone the size of New Jersey.

Climate change will only make pollution worse. Increased rainfall intensity will cause more runoff. The U.S. Environmental Protection Agency (EPA) expects that in the future more waterways will be considered "impaired." That means fewer fish to eat, less water to drink, and more disease.

CHANGING ATTITUDES

Complicating and slowing the urgent fight against climate change is the fact that many Americans don't believe human activity is even responsible for global warming. Thirty-six percent think global warming is happening naturally, and 10 percent don't believe in global warming at all. Only 47 percent of Americans think global warming is a serious problem. Thirty-five percent believe there's genuine disagreement

REVISITING NUCLEAR POWER

Most power plants heat water to create steam. The steam pushes a turbine that in turn generates electricity. Different types of power plants use different methods to heat water. A nuclear power plant uses a process called fission in which one atom splits into two and releases energy. Nuclear power plants emit much less CO_2 than coal power plants. They also produce about a million times more energy per unit weight than fossil fuels.

The American public is split on nuclear power for a few reasons. First, nuclear power plants use uranium because its atoms are unstable. The instability makes uranium atoms easier to break in two, yet it also causes uranium to spontaneously release energy in the form of radiation, which is harmful to living things. Once the uranium is used, radioactive waste remains. It can't be destroyed, so it has to be stored safely, monitored, and guarded.

Also, if something malfunctions, the nuclear reactor—the device in the power plant that causes fission—can overheat, explode, and pollute the environment with radiation. Food and water supplies can become radiated. A few such accidents have caused widespread, lasting damage to the surrounding areas, occasionally poisoning nearby citizens with radiation.

However, there have only been a few such accidents in all of history. Fossil fuels are actually more dangerous. In fact, from 1931 to 1995, coal mining has killed over thirty-three thousand people, but in the United States, no one is known to have died from a nuclear power accident or resulting radiation-related health problems. Oil spills have caused irreparable damage to ecosystems.

Nuclear power is actually safer and cleaner than burning fossil fuels. Experts believe that to limit climate change and meet increasing demand, we may need to rely on nuclear power in the future.

within the scientific community about climate change and human responsibility for it. This is untrue, however; 84 percent of scientists have concluded that humans cause global warming, and 70 percent think it's a serious problem.

Why can't we agree? It could be because climate change has become a highly politicized issue. The disagreement is drawn down party lines: 67 percent of Republicans don't believe humans contribute to climate change, but 64 percent of Democrats do. The argument is typically about ideology and money. Big business and the politicians it funds do not like the prospect of potentially expensive "green" changes to standard, fossil fuel–based industry practice. The argument is rarely only about cold, hard facts and actual science. The lack of common ground between political parties and their supporters makes it extremely difficult to orchestrate a concerted and effective war against global warming and climate change.

Unfortunately, at the present moment, the global economy still requires fossil fuels for its power, and the petroleum, coal, and natural gas industries are all enormous,

As fuel prices rise, so do the prices of transported food and manufactured and shipped goods. This is just one way that climate change already affects our daily lives.

politically influential, and well-connected. Fuel companies use their money and influence to persuade politicians to support their best interests. Needless to say, they're more concerned with profit than with the short-term or long-term environmental impact of their policies and practices.

Many Americans can't yet see how climate change will affect them, so they're reluctant to alter their way of life. But it's starting to make financial sense to "go green." Fuel prices are rising. That means that prices go up not just for gasoline, but for everything. Trucks, planes, trains, and cargo ships all use fossil fuels to transport people and goods, including food. If a business has to pay more for shipping because of rising fuel costs, it'll pass that cost on to the consumer. As fuel gets more expensive, so will food. It's unlikely that we'll be able to ignore climate change for long.

CHAPTER three

Safeguarding Food and Water Supplies Today

Concerned individuals and organizations all around the world are working hard to find practical ways to limit the human impact upon global warming and climate change while also safeguarding food and water supplies. Many climate change projects—from the highly local to the global—are already in operation, completed, or ready to begin.

EPA water quality experts collect floodwater samples for water quality and contamination tests in New Orleans, Louisiana.

GOVERNMENT REGULATIONS

The U.S. Environmental Protection Agency is a governmental agency responsible for protecting the environment and human health by creating regulations and enforcing them. The EPA's regulations attempt to limit the negative impact an individual or business can have on the environment. For example, the EPA enforces a certain standard of air and water quality in an effort to prevent excessive pollution. In doing so, EPA regulations also help limit the human contribution to climate change.

INTERNATIONAL TREATIES

Climate change is a global problem. The Kyoto Protocol is the United Nations' groundbreaking international environmental treaty signed in 1997 in Kyoto, Japan. It binds nearly every industrialized nation, except the United States, to reduce greenhouse gas emissions.

Why hasn't the United States signed the Kyoto Protocol? The Kyoto Protocol doesn't apply to poorer countries called "developing nations." Since the treaty was signed, certain nations that were once considered "developing," like China, Brazil, and India, have become relatively wealthy and heavily industrialized. Todd Stern, President Barack Obama's climate change envoy to the United Nations, says it isn't fair that these countries keep their special status even though they now have huge industrial economies that contribute significantly to climate change.

The provisions of the Kyoto Protocol end in 2012. The United Nations continues to meet and discuss a new climate change treaty for the future. So far, there's no new international agreement.

CLEAN, RENEWABLE ENERGY

Renewable energy comes from resources that are naturally replenished, like wind, water, or the sun. Fossil fuels, on the other hand, cannot be naturally replenished—once they're gone, they're gone. In this way, renewable energy sources can protect us from unexpected energy shortages or rising oil prices. Certain renewable energy sources are also considered clean because they don't release greenhouse gases into the atmosphere or contribute to global warming. Solar energy and wind power are both examples of clean, renewable energy sources.

Turbines like these can harness the wind to generate energy that is both clean and renewable.

Currently, renewable energy sources account for 8 percent of the United States' supply. We don't use more green energy because renewable energy plants are expensive to build and maintain in the short term. They also usually have to be in geographically remote locations where the energy source and space are most abundant. For example, solar power plants are often built in deserts where sunlight is both reliable and plentiful. Because the plants are often far from the communities they serve, electricity transmission lines must be built over long distances.

In the future, however, we will use more renewable energy, thanks to tax credits and government initiatives that encourage renewable energy projects by driving costs down. Most people agree on the long-term benefits of renewable energy, if only to promote energy independence (not having to rely on other countries for fuel supplies). Climate change and shrinking supplies of fossil fuels will force the issue. There's enormous potential for clean renewables to support our energy needs in the future. A happy by-product of greater reliance upon renewable energy sources will be food and water supplies untainted by toxins and less saddled with high transportation costs.

WATER CONSERVATION

Even though the U.S. population has grown, water consumption hasn't increased correspondingly in the past few years. That's all due to new technology, new laws, and public awareness campaigns. Even so, Americans still use too much water—about twice as much as the world's average. In 2005, the United States consumed about 410 billion gallons (1.5 trillion liters) of water per day. That's because the average American way of life requires more resources than in most other parts of the world.

Every year, about 240,000 outdated water mains break. Those breaks contaminate and waste drinking water and cause damage, like flooding. The EPA estimates that 7 billion gallons (26.5 billion liters) of clean drinking water are lost every day because of broken or leaky pipes. In the future, increased rainfall will push our aging water infrastructure to the limit, resulting in even more frequent water main breaks. The American Recovery and Reinvestment Act of 2009 pledged $6 billion for water projects, including those that would update our water infrastructure. Unfortunately, it's not nearly enough. The EPA estimates that it will cost $335 billion to fix America's water infrastructure over the next twenty years. In the years ahead, when water shortages become more common due to climate change, it is likely that billions of gallons of freshwater will continue to be contaminated or wasted because of a degraded water system.

At this point, the best way to protect our water supply is to use less. Engineering can help us in this effort. There are some new technologies and methods that are making it even easier to conserve water. Some people use gray water— wastewater from household activities, like dishwashing, bathing, or laundry that can be recycled for use on lawns

A broken main spews thousands of gallons of water onto a highway in Connecticut. In the United States, 7 billion gallons (26.5 billion liters) of clean drinking water a day are lost due to broken or leaky pipes.

or gardens or to flush toilets. Gray water doesn't contain any human waste, but it isn't clean enough to drink. New, specially designed plumbing systems can collect and store gray water in homes and businesses. Gray water relieves the growing pressure on water systems by reducing freshwater demand and usage and decreasing the amount of water flowing to treatment plants.

Rain barrels, or rainwater tanks, also help conserve water by collecting and storing rainfall and runoff. That water can be used to water gardens, flush toilets, or even for drinking if it's properly filtered and cleaned. It might seem like it would be a time-consuming and expensive undertaking to buy and install a rain barrel, but many people use small, inexpensive containers to collect rain. Even something as humble and basic as empty milk jugs, for example, can effectively harvest rain. Even suburbanites and urban gardeners are increasingly using specially designed rain barrels that are covered and attached by hosing to storm gutters. Many people use open rain barrels in rural areas around the world. The downside is that these improvised, coverless rain barrels collect less water and are vulnerable to bugs that lay eggs in standing water, like mosquitoes.

The turf grass that is used on lawns across America is the largest irrigated crop in the United States. Given the amount of water and chemical fertilizer needed to maintain a green lawn in the heat of summer, it seems increasingly unnecessary and irresponsible to waste precious resources and introduce chemicals into the soil and water table just for the sake of one half acre (2,023 square meters) of green grass.

WILL ALLEN AND URBAN AGRICULTURE

Lower-income families can't always afford to buy organic or local food at higher costs. On top of that, in many places it's hard to find healthy produce of any kind, be it organic, local, or conventional. We call these places food deserts. They're in both rural and urban areas, mostly in lower-income and minority neighborhoods. People who live in food deserts have to rely on whatever is available, usually processed fast or frozen food, which, when eaten to excess, causes health problems like diabetes and heart disease. Thankfully, people like Will Allen are attempting to "green" these food deserts.

Allen is a former professional basketball player who loves to farm. Later in life, he bought a foreclosed plant nursery in a food desert in Milwaukee, Wisconsin, and redesigned it for use in urban agriculture. He sold his produce at farmers' markets and in the neighborhood. Eventually, Allen started giving classes to neighborhood kids who wanted to learn how to grow food. More and more people wanted to learn. It was the beginning of Growing Power.

Growing Power is Allen's nonprofit organization that helps communities create sustainable food systems. The farm in Milwaukee is urban agriculture at its finest, most efficient, and most sustainable. It features fourteen greenhouses packed closely on 2 acres (8,094 square meters) of land, only half a mile (0.8 kilometers) from Milwaukee's largest public housing project. Allen's urban farm maximizes space, growing as much food as possible using sustainable, all-natural methods. The farm also has beehives and even livestock and fish: chicken, duck, turkey, and tilapia. Growing Power is bringing healthy produce to food deserts and spreading the word about sustainable urban agriculture.

Thankfully, there are nonprofit organizations, community gardens, and co-ops all around the country doing work similar to that of Growing Power. Look in your area to get involved. "We need 50 million more people growing food," Will Allen told the *New York Times*, "on porches, in pots, in side yards."

Xeriscape landscapes are designed to reduce or eliminate the need for irrigation. They use planning, soil analysis, plant selection, and efficient irrigation to promote water conservation and pollution prevention. Xeriscape landscapes also take less time and effort to maintain. They're promoted in over forty states, especially in regions that don't have access to reliable water sources, like the American Southwest. Using gray water and rain barrels can also help limit the enormously wasteful impact of watering lawns.

GREEN BUILDING

Boulder, Colorado, is becoming America's first Smart Grid City. Fifty thousand households are being upgraded with the latest environmentally friendly, energy-saving technology like solar panels and electric cars. Monitoring systems will track and report precise data on each household's carbon footprint, allowing families to chart their energy consumption, identify the areas of greatest waste, and make the necessary adjustments to reduce it. Boulder is now a prototype "green city"

The Bank of America Tower in New York City is a fine example of green architecture. It's one of the most energy-efficient and environmentally friendly buildings in the world.

for the rest of America and the world.

Increasingly, architects and city planners are designing buildings with the environment in mind. Sustainable buildings are cost-effective in the long run because they use less energy. They use natural processes of heat and ventilation, rather than electricity. They can even incorporate small-scale renewable energy generation, like solar panels or wind turbines, so as not to rely on fossil fuel power plants.

The Bank of America Tower is one such building. The second-tallest building in New York City, it was designed by Cook+Fox Architects to be one of the most energy-efficient, environmentally friendly buildings in the world. The building has rain barrels on the roof and a gray water plumbing system. In the bathroom, waterless urinals are expected to save 8 million gallons (30,283,296 liters) of water per year. Its windows are made of insulated glass that helps control the interior climate. It was also built using recycled materials.

CHAPTER four

Safeguarding Food and Water Supplies Tomorrow

Think of how much the world has changed in just the past decade. Now think of what things will be like ten years from now. It's impossible to know, but one thing is certain—technology will continue to advance at a rapid pace. There are many climate change–related threats to food and water supplies in the near- and long-term future, but there are even more mitigation and adaptation solutions on the horizon.

Some of them sound like science fiction, but one day they may be very real and help preserve our access to safe and reliable food and water supplies.

INVENTIONS AND INNOVATIONS

Engineers have invented "artificial trees," structures that absorb carbon dioxide just like a tree does. These buildings use a special resin to which carbon clings. When the resin is wet, it releases the CO_2, which can be stored, preventing it from being emitted into the atmosphere where it will trap the sun's heat. The captured CO_2 can be sold to businesses that need it, like soda companies or greenhouses. This technology already exists, but it's not yet cost effective. As the need grows and demand for such a solution increases, the cost will probably come down as the volume of artificial tree production will climb.

What if we could reflect heat from the sun back into space? Some scientists have suggested building a giant screen of crisscrossed aluminum strands. The screen would be carried into space by a rocket or spacecraft and released. Once situated, it would repel infrared radiation, but not completely keep the sun's light and heat from reaching Earth. It would be an extremely difficult undertaking, considering how big the screen would need to be and how challenging its design, construction, placement, and maintenance would be. Using the same principle, however, we could also try a more earthbound approach. Icy regions around the world could be blanketed with reflectors. Certain specially designed blankets are already used in the Alps to protect ski hills from melting in the summer. This would be a large-scale version of that practice, designed to reflect the sun's heat away from the planetary surface.

Reforestation is a great way to remove and absorb carbon from the atmosphere and limit habitat loss from deforestation, but it can be a time-consuming and expensive process. Why plant one tree at a time when you can just drop a seed bomb? Tree bombs can be dropped from planes. When they

GEOENGINEERING

Humans manipulate the environment in many ways, both intentionally and unintentionally. Global warming is an example of an unintentional—and extremely negative—manipulation of the environment and global climate by humans. Yet humans can also attempt to manipulate the environment in a positive way, in a manner that will actually counteract global warming and climate change. We call this geoengineering.

There are many possibilities for geoengineering—some not yet thought of; some we already practice or have tested. For example, if we injected sulfur particles into the upper atmosphere, they would reflect the sun's heat and cool the planet. We know this would work because it's happened before; when volcanoes spew sulfuric acid into the air, the sulfur particles temporarily cool the surrounding area. We currently have the technology to attempt this on a large scale. If it worked, it would be a fast, cheap, and effective way to combat global warming.

explode, they disperse seeds across a wide area. This could become a much quicker, easier, cheaper, more efficient, and less labor-intensive way to plant trees and create huge carbon sinks.

THE FUTURE OF FOOD

Experts are trying to invent new ways to protect the world's food supplies and maximize future production, all while limiting agriculture's impact on the environment. For example, scientists are working hard to develop climate change–resistant crops. These crops would be better suited to the higher temperatures and variable precipitation expected in the future. That way, food production wouldn't drop off drastically, even if the consequences of climate change are as harsh as some computer models suggest.

Recently, scientists at the John Innes Centre in Norwich, England, discovered the "thermometer gene" in plants. This gene helps plants sense temperature. By taking away a certain plant protein, agricultural scientists could manipulate the gene and trick the plant's sense of temperature, making it more tolerant to hotter weather. This finding could pave the way for climate change–resistant crops sometime in the future.

Someday, you might drink milk from a cloned cow. Cloning is very attractive because it gives farmers complete control over their livestock's genes. Through cloning, they could also enrich milk and meat with vitamins and nutrients, which would help solve the world's massive and persistent malnutrition problem. The U.S. Food and Drug Administration (FDA), which sets standards for food quality, has already approved

Demonstrators protest the FDA's decision to allow the sale of meat and milk from cloned cows, pigs, and goats. Though they may seem unnatural, the FDA insists that the meat and dairy products derived from cloned livestock are as safe as those provided by non-cloned animals.

food and milk from cloned cattle, pigs, and goats. According to the FDA, food from these cloned animals is just as safe as food from non-cloned ones.

Another way in which farming may soon change is in its locale. So-called urban farms—mostly small plots of land reclaimed from abandoned lots—have been growing in popularity in recent years. Yet urban farming may soon be moving up in the world—way up. Vertical farming is urban agriculture at its most extreme. Many people believe that it's more efficient and environmentally responsible to farm inside of skyscrapers using green growing methods. That way, farmers can maximize the amount grown within a certain area of land—by growing upward rather than growing outward—while using energy-efficient and eco-friendly agricultural practices, including the elimination of toxic chemical runoff, water waste, and soil depletion.

Farms can be major producers of greenhouse gases, particularly methane. Cows contribute to climate change by releasing methane in their manure and flatulence (digestive gas). To fix that problem, some scientists have suggested feeding cows garlic. As strange as it sounds, garlic kills methane-producing bacteria in cows' stomachs, thereby cutting their greenhouse gas emissions!

THE FUTURE OF FRESHWATER

What if we could control the rain and generate precipitation whenever we needed to replenish our dwindling freshwater supplies? Far-fetched as it sounds, this might actually be possible. When silver iodide or dry ice (frozen carbon dioxide) particles are dropped on clouds from above, precipitation increases, possibly by 10 to 15 percent. It's actually been used before to end droughts. Cloud seeding, as it's called, could have unintended consequences, however. In 2009, cloud seeding seems to have caused a sudden blizzard in China. Perhaps one day, it will be a more carefully controlled

Skyscraper farming

A futuristic concept converts skyscrapers into crop farms that could help reduce global warming, improve urban environment, and feed the world's growing population; how it would work:

Solar panel

Energy supplied by a rotating solar panel that follows sun; drives interior cooling/heating system

Glass panels

Clear coating of titanium oxide collects pollutants, makes rain slide down the glass where it is collected and used for watering

Architecture

Circular design allows maximum light into center

Economy

Combines farming with office and residential stories

Irrigation

Filtered, sterilized wastewater from sewage system can be used for irrigation

© 2008 MCT
Source: Vertical Farm project
Graphic: Morten Lyhne, Elsebeth Nielsen

Though it sounds like science fiction, skyscraper farming could soon revolutionize agriculture by maximizing food production, minimizing pollution and carbon emissions, and utilizing very small amounts of space and precious natural resources like freshwater.

and reliable science. Countries in dry parts of the world are researching the possibilities.

If we're running low on water, why not turn to the vast water resources surrounding every continent? Desalination is a process whereby salt and other minerals are removed from ocean water to make it drinkable. At first glance, it may seem like it would solve all of our water supply problems, but desalination accounts for only 1 percent of current global water usage. Why? It's not suited for inland or high-altitude areas that are far from oceans and that would require long-distance transport of the desalinated water. And it's expensive. Desalination plants require enormous amounts of energy to function, and if that energy is produced by fossil fuels, it will contribute to climate change. Desalination technology is improving, however, and there is the potential to use renewable energy sources to desalinate water in the future. That would prevent emissions and make desalination cheaper in the long run. Currently, the Middle East uses about 70 percent of the world's desalinated water. The United States uses desalinated water in dry coastal states like California.

CHAPTER five

Do Your Part

Climate change and global warming are long-term, multigenerational, worldwide problems. The challenges are so daunting and complex, and the process so advanced, that it's hard to see how scientists, governments, and organizations can do anything to stem and reverse the tide. But what about you? As surprising as it may seem, there is much you can do to fight climate change, primarily by shrinking your carbon footprint and living a sustainable life. All it takes is some knowledge, effort, and consideration.

A leaky faucet can waste 10,000 gallons (37,854 liters) of water every year.

A SUSTAINABLE DAILY LIFE

One of the best ways to limit your impact on the environment is to conserve precious and nonrenewable resources and consume less of everything. Do your best to use less water, less energy, and fewer packaged goods. It's all interconnected—power plants use water, water treatment facilities use electricity, and manufacturers use both water and electricity.

It's easy to conserve water. Turn off the tap when you're brushing your teeth or washing dishes. Take showers instead of baths, and make them quick. If you notice a leaky faucet, tell your parents and get it fixed. Leaks can account for 10,000 gallons (37,854 liters) of wasted water every year. That's enough to fill a swimming pool.

Don't use bottled water unless you have to. Some people think bottled water is healthier than tap water, but that's not true. In fact, it could be the opposite because government standards for and regulation of bottled water are not as strict. Bottled water is also much more expensive and generates lots of plastic waste. Try a water filter or filtered pitcher

FOOD WASTE

The United Nations says that one-third of global food production is lost or wasted. That's 1.3 billion tons of food, not to mention the water, labor, money, and energy that went into its production. Food loss and waste are a big cause of food insecurity around the world. Do your best not to waste food. Talk to your parents about planning your grocery purchases so that you buy only what's needed. If you have more than you can eat, bring extra food to homeless shelters or food banks in your area.

instead—they're cheap ways to make sure that your water is clean. If you have to buy bottled water, buy big bottles to limit your trash. Reusable containers are always better than disposable. A thermos or aluminum water bottle, for example, is a great, permanent alternative to a disposable plastic bottle.

When you make trash, recycle what you can. There are recycling programs all around the country that collect certain materials in trash so they can be reused. Sort your aluminum, plastic, and paper goods. The symbol of three arrows chasing one another in a triangle shows that something is both recyclable and made of recycled materials, but it doesn't necessarily mean you can recycle it in your area. Different cities have different rules. Check your hometown's recycling and sanitation Web site for information.

Conserving electricity will limit water usage and the amount of fossil fuels your local power plant burns. Turn off lights and electronics when you don't need them. Plugged-in appliances, especially those with electronic displays or clocks, actually drain small amounts of electricity even when they're turned off, so if you go on a trip, unplug your appliances. Replace your lightbulbs with new, more energy-efficient compact fluorescent ones. You can save gasoline by walking, riding your bike, carpooling, or taking public transportation whenever possible.

CONVENTIONAL VS. ORGANIC

You've most likely seen organic food in your supermarket. What does "organic" mean? According to the U.S. Department of Agriculture (USDA), "Organic is a labeling term that indicates that the food or other agricultural product has been produced through approved methods that integrate cultural, biological, and mechanical practices that foster cycling of resources, promote ecological balance, and conserve biodiversity." That means no genetic enhancements, synthetic fertilizers, hormones, or chemical pesticides or herbicides.

It's important to know how your food is grown and where it comes from. Most fruits and vegetables are packaged and shipped over long distances before they reach your shelf. Delivery trucks and cargo ships burn fossil fuels and release greenhouse gases into the atmosphere. It's best to buy from local, organic, sustainable, small-scale farmers who care about their environmental impact. Their produce, meat, and eggs may be slightly more expensive, but your money will support a local, responsible business, not a corporation

It's best to buy produce from organic, environmentally conscious growers. The food and soil are pesticide-free. The produce has not traveled far, so its carbon footprint is small. And local farmers are supported in their efforts to maintain biodiversity by planting, harvesting, and selling heirloom varieties of fruits and vegetables.

concerned more about profit than about food quality, consumer safety, and environmental protection and sustainability. Check the labels next time you're in the grocery store.

YOUR LOCAL FOOD SYSTEM

Talk to your family about supporting your local ecosystem and economy by buying locally grown food. Buying locally limits transportation-related carbon emissions and promotes food biodiversity, since many small farmers grow local food varieties. Shop at a farmers' market where local growers sell their produce.

Eating less meat is another way to help the environment. Livestock require large amounts of food and water, not to mention grazing land cleared of trees—all of which stress the environment. If you do eat meat, try to get it from an environmentally conscious farm, one that not only uses sound ecological practices, but also uses grass feed and does not inject its cows with hormones.

If you're interested in learning how to grow—and perhaps even sell—your own produce, get involved with a community garden, co-op, or food project. If one does not yet exist, start one yourself and launch a green and local food revolution in your own neighborhood.

GET INVOLVED

If you're interested, you can learn more about growing food. There are many community gardens and co-ops that provide classes. Learning about where food comes from is a great way to stay healthy and prepare for climate change. If you live in a city, there are plenty of urban agricultural organizations, rooftop gardens, and greenhouses sprouting up all around the country. And if you want to do more, help plant trees locally and consider growing your own vegetable garden or joining a community garden.

Find out more about the area you live in. What type of power plant generates your electricity? How old is your water system? How clean is your water? Does your city allow gray water systems? Where does your food come from? The more you know, the more informed your decision making can be about how to create a more sustainable life. Look for local environmental organizations to join, volunteer, or donate to. If you disagree with local, state, or national policies, write to your mayor, state representative, or senator.

Spread the word about the importance of reducing one's carbon footprint and leading an environmentally sustainable lifestyle. Talk to your friends. Visit informative Web sites like GreenMyParents.com for ideas on how to convince your parents to go green. You can do a lot alone, but you can do even more together. Most of all, set a good example. If you inspire five people, and each of them inspires five others, you could start a chain reaction and launch a green revolution. Climate change is frightening, but we can take control of the situation and turn the tide, starting with the way we lead our daily lives.

GLOSsary

adapt To adjust to changing circumstances or conditions and continue to flourish. In terms of climate change, to alter human behavior to respond to the negative effects of climate change.

carbon footprint The total amount of greenhouse gas emissions caused by an individual or organization.

carbon offset A reduction in greenhouse gas emissions made to compensate for emissions elsewhere.

carbon sink Anything that collects and stores carbon, such as forests and oceans.

climate change Lasting changes in temperature and weather patterns.

dead zone Low-oxygen area in oceans and waterways where fish and aquatic plant life is difficult to sustain.

fission Nuclear reaction in which the nucleus of an atom splits and releases energy. Used in nuclear power plants.

food desert An area in an industrialized country in which healthy, affordable food is difficult to find.

fossil fuel Nonrenewable energy source like oil, coal, or natural gas that releases greenhouse gases, particularly carbon dioxide, when burned.

geoengineering Purposely manipulating the environment to counteract the effects of climate change and global warming.

global warming The rising of average world surface and ocean temperatures.

gray water Recycled wastewater from household activities that can be used to water gardens and lawns and flush toilets.

greenhouse effect The process whereby radiation from the sun is absorbed and reradiated by greenhouse gases in the atmosphere, resulting in global surface temperatures warm enough to sustain life.

Green Revolution The period of increased agriculture production, beginning in the 1960s, because of technological advances.

Industrial Revolution The period from the eighteenth through the nineteenth centuries during which technological advances transformed industry and daily life and resulted in the first large-scale emissions of fossil fuels.

mitigation The act of decreasing the impact of human activities that are resulting in global warming and climate change.

nonpoint source An indirect source of pollution.

organic food Food produced through natural methods, without synthetic pesticides, chemical fertilizers, hormones, or genetically modified organisms.

renewable energy Energy from naturally replenished sources, such as wind, sun, and water.

yield The amount of something produced, such as crops.

FOR MORE INFORmation

Canadian Wildlife Federation
350 Michael Cowpland Drive
Kanata, ON K2M 2W1
Canada
(800) 563-9453
Web site: http://www.cwf-fcf.org
The Canadian Wildlife Federation is Canada's largest non-
    profit organization that protects plants, animals, and
    habitats in Canada.

Environment Canada
Inquiry Centre
10 Wellington, 23rd Floor
Gatineau QC K1A 0H3
Canada
(819) 997-2800
Web site: http://www.ec.gc.ca
Environment Canada is the department of the government of
    Canada that is in charge of protecting and enhancing the
    environment.

Freshwater Future
P.O. Box 2479
Petoskey, MI 49770
(231) 348-8200
Freshwater Future builds effective community-based citi-
    zen action to protect and restore the water quality of
    the Great Lakes basin. It works toward this goal by
    providing financial assistance, communications and net-
    working assistance, and technical assistance to citizens
    and grassroots watershed groups throughout the Great
    Lakes basin.

Growing Power
5500 West Silver Spring Drive
Milwaukee, WI 53218
(414) 527-1546
Web site: http://www.growingpower.org
Growing Power supports the development of sustainable
community food systems.

National Oceanic and Atmospheric Administration (NOAA)
1401 Constitution Avenue NW, Room 5128
Washington, DC 20230
Web site: http://www.noaa.gov
The NOAA is a scientific agency within the U.S. Department
of Commerce concerned with the conditions of the
oceans and the atmosphere.

U.S. Department of Energy
1000 Independence Avenue SW
Washington, DC 20585
(202) 586-5000
Web site: http://www.energy.gov
This is the cabinet-level department responsible for energy
policies and safety.

U.S. Environmental Protection Agency (EPA)
Ariel Rios Building
1200 Pennsylvania Avenue NW
Washington, DC 20460
(202) 272-0167
Web site: http://www.epa.gov
The EPA protects the environment and human health by
writing and enforcing regulations.

WEB SITES

Due to the changing nature of Internet links, Rosen Publishing has developed an online list of Web sites related to the subject of this book. This site is updated regularly. Please use this link to access the list:

http://www.rosenlinks.com/sttr/supp

Bradman, Tony. *Under the Weather: Stories About Climate Change*. London, England: Frances Lincoln Children's Books, 2010.

Casper, Julie Kerr. *The Food We Grow and Animals We Raise*. New York, NY: Chelsea House Publications, 2007.

Evans, Kate. *Weird Weather: Everything You Didn't Want to Know About Climate Change but Probably Should Find Out*. Toronto, ON, Canada: Groundwood Books, 2007.

Freeman, S. David. *Winning Our Energy Independence: An Energy Insider Shows How*. Layton, UT: Gibbs Smith, 2007.

Hall, Julie. *A Hot Planet Needs Cool Kids: Understanding Climate Change and What You Can Do About It*. Bainbridge Island, WA: Green Goat Books, 2007.

Johanson, Paula. *Jobs in Sustainable Agriculture*. New York, NY: Rosen Publishing Group, 2010.

Johnson, Rebecca L. *Investigating Climate Change: Scientists' Search for Answers in a Warming World*. Minneapolis, MN: Twenty-First Century Books, 2008.

Kaplan, Rachel. *Urban Homesteading: Heirloom Skills for Sustainable Living*. New York, NY: Skyhorse Publishing, 2011.

Kaye, Cathryn Berger. *A Kid's Guide to Climate Change & Global Warming: How to Take Action!* Minneapolis, MN: Free Spirit Publishing, 2009.

La Bella, Laura. *Not Enough to Drink: Pollution, Drought, and Tainted Water Supplies*. New York, NY: Rosen Publishing Group, 2009.

McCutcheon, Chuck. *What Are Global Warming and Climate Change?: Answers for Young Readers*. Albuquerque, NM: University of New Mexico Press, 2010.

Prud'homme, Alex. *The Ripple Effect*. New York, NY: Scribner, 2011.

Sivertsen, Linda. *Generation Green: The Ultimate Teen Guide to Living an Eco-Friendly Life*. New York, NY: Simon Pulse, 2008.

Spilsbury, Richard. *Ask an Expert: Climate Change.* New York, NY: Crabtree Publishing Company, 2010.

Stec, Laura. *Cool Cuisine: Taking the Bite Out of Global Warming*. Layton, UT: Gibbs Smith, 2008.

Stracher, Cameron. *The Water Wars.* Naperville, IL: Sourcebooks Fire, 2011.

Strauss, Rochelle. *One Well: The Story of Water on Earth*. Tonawanda, NY: Kids Can Press, 2007.

Tabak, John. *Wind and Water*. New York, NY: Facts On File, 2009.

Taylor, Nancy H. *Go Green: How to Build an Earth-Friendly Community*. Layton, UT: Gibbs Smith, 2008.

Walker, Sally M. *We Are the Weather Makers: The History of Climate Change*. Somerville, MA: Candlewick, 2009.

Ahrens, C. Donald, and Perry J. Samson. *Extreme Weather and Climate*. Belmont, CA: Brooks/Cole, 2010.

Biello, David. "Fertilizer Runoff Overwhelms Streams and Rivers—Creating Vast 'Dead Zones.'" *Scientific American*, March 14, 2008. Retrieved September 2011 (http://www.scientificamerican.com/article .cfm?id=fertilizer-runoff-overwhelms-streams).

CNN. "Organic vs. Conventional: What Do Experts Say?" April 13, 2007. Retrieved September 2011 (http://articles.cnn.com/2007-04-13/health/ cl.organics_1_organic-foods-organic-products-organic-market?_s=PM:HEALTH).

Congressional Budget Office. *Potential Impacts of Climate Change in the United States*. Washington, DC: Congressional Budget Office, 2009.

Cullen, Heidi. *The Weather of the Future: Heat Waves, Extreme Storms, and Other Scenes from a Climate-Changed Planet*. New York, NY: Harper, 2010.

Delano, Marfe Ferguson. *Earth in the Hot Seat: Bulletins from a Warming World*. Des Moines, IA: National Geographic Children's Books, 2009.

Evans, Robert. "New Green Farming Vital to End Global Hunger." Reuters, July 5, 2011. Retrieved September 2011 (http://www.reuters.com/article/2011/07/05/ us-un-farms-idUSTRE7641MT20110705).

Food and Agriculture Organization of the United States. "The Green Revolution." Retrieved September 2011 (http://www.fao.org/kids/en/revolution.html).

Goldenberg, Suzanne. "Most Americans Unconvinced Humans Responsible for Climate Change, Study Finds." *Guardian*, July 9, 2009. Retrieved September 2011 (http://www.guardian.co.uk/environment/2009/jul/09/ climate-change-debate-human-activity).

Kahn, Michael. "Model Sees Severe Climate Change Impact by 2050." Reuters, February 12, 2009. Retrieved September 2011 (http://www.reuters.com/article/2009/02/13/us-climate-model-idUSTRE51C03920090213).

Keith, David. "David Keith's Unusual Climate Change Idea." TED, September 2007. Retrieved September 2011 (http://www.ted.com/talks/david_keith_s_surprising_ideas_on_climate_change.html).

Kosik, Alison. "Experts: U.S. Water Infrastructure in Trouble." CNN, January 21, 2011. Retrieved September 2011 (http://www.cnn.com/2011/US/01/20/water.main.infrastructure/index.html).

Kunzig, Robert. "Population Seven Billion." *National Geographic*, Vol. 219, No. 1, January 2011, pp. 32-69.

Morris, Nigel. "Climate Change Could Force 1 Billion from Their Homes by 2050." *Independent*, April 29, 2008. Retrieved September 2011 (http://www.independent.co.uk/environment/climate-change/climate-change-could-force-1-billion-from-their-homes-by-2050-817223.html).

NASA. "Climate Change: Evidence." Retrieved September 2011 (http://climate.nasa.gov/evidence).

PBS. "Greenhouse–Green Planet." Retrieved September 2011 (http://www.pbs.org/wgbh/nova/ice/greenhouse.html).

Pepper, Daniel. "The Toxic Consequences of the Green Revolution." *U.S. News and World Report*, July 7, 2008. Retrieved September 2011 (http://www.usnews.com/news/world/articles/2008/07/07/the-toxic-consequences-of-the-green-revolution).

Prud'homme, Alex. *The Ripple Effect*. New York, NY: Scribner, 2011.

Royte, Elizabeth. "The Street Farmer." *New York Times,* July 1, 2009. Retrieved September 2011 (http://www .nytimes.com/2009/07/05/magazine/05allen-t .html?pagewanted=all).

Siebert, Charles. "Food Ark." *National Geographic*, Vol. 220, No.1, July 2011, pp. 108-131.

U.S. Department of Energy. "Fossil Energy: How Fossil Fuels Were Formed." Retrieved September 2011 (http:// www.fe.doe.gov/education/energylessons/coal/gen_ howformed.html).

U.S. Environmental Protection Agency. "Climate Change: Basic Information." Retrieved August 2011 (http://www .epa.gov/climatechange/basicinfo.html).

U.S. Environmental Protection Agency. "U.S. Greenhouse Gas Inventory." Retrieved August 2011 (http://www.epa .gov/climatechange/emissions/usgginventory.html).

U.S. Environmental Protection Agency. "Water Resources." Retrieved September 2011 (http://www.epa.gov/ climatechange/effects/water).

Ward, Diane Raines. *Water Wars: Drought, Flood, Folly, and the Politics of Thirst*. New York, NY: Riverhead Books, 2002.

Ward, Peter Douglas. *The Flooded Earth: Our Future in a World Without Ice Caps*. New York, NY: Basic Books, 2010.

INDex

A

Allen, Will, 34–35
artificial trees, 38

C

climate change, 4–6, 7–8, 12–13, 26
  disagreement about, 23–26
  effect on food production, 14
  effect on water supplies, 14–16
  efforts to slow, 6, 16, 17–20, 25,
    27–31, 37–40
  what you can do to limit, 45,
    46–48, 51
cloning of livestock, 40–41

D

desalination of ocean water, 44
droughts, 4–5, 14, 15–16, 20, 42

E

energy, conserving, 47–48
Environmental Protection Agency
  (EPA), 23, 28, 31, 32

F

famine, 4, 5, 12, 20
farming practices, rethinking, 19–20
floods, 14, 15–16
food biodiversity, 18–19, 50
food supplies and production
  effect of climate change on, 14

  efforts to protect, 40–42
  and food waste, 47
  threat to, 4, 5, 8
fossil fuels, 10–11, 13, 25–26, 29,
  31, 36, 44, 47, 48
freshwater
  effect of climate change on, 14–16
  future of, 42–44

G

genetic engineering of crops and
  livestock, 18
geoengineering, 39
global warming, 5–6, 7–8, 29, 45
  doubts about, 23–25
  and human activity, 10–13,
    23–26, 39
government regulations, 28
green building, 35–36
greenhouse effect, 8–10
greenhouse gases, 8–10, 11, 13, 15,
  18, 29, 42
Green Revolution, 12, 18, 20
Growing Power, 34–35

H

heat waves, 7, 14
human activity
  doubts about it causing global
    warming, 23–25
  effect on food and water supplies,
    5–6, 7–16
  and global warming/climate change,
    10–13, 23–26, 28

I

international treaties, 28–29

K

Kyoto Protocol, 28–29

L

locally grown foods, purchasing, 48, 49–50

M

malnourishment worldwide, 4, 20

N

nonpoint water pollution, 21–23
nuclear power, 24–25

O

organic food, 48–49

R

recycling, 47
renewable energy, 29–31, 36, 44
runoff, 16, 22–23, 42

S

seed bombs, 39–40
stem rust fungus, 19
sustainable daily life, living a, 46–48, 51
Svalbard Global Seed Vault, 6

U

United Nations, 4, 20, 28–29
urban farming, 34–35, 41–42

W

water conservation efforts, 6, 31–35, 46
water pollution, 21–23
water supplies
    effect of climate change on, 14–16
    efforts to protect, 42–44
threat to, 4, 5, 8

ABOUT THE AUTHOR

Joe Craig is an author who has written previously about teens, society, and technology.

PHOTO CREDITS

Cover, pp. 1, 3, 4–5 © www.istockphoto.com/Jon Schulte; p. 5 Ali Al-Saadi/AFP/Getty Images; p. 9 Roy Flooks/ Getty Images; p. 11 Hemera/Thinkstock; pp. 15, 19, 32, 50 © AP Images; p. 21 Otto Bakano/AFP/Getty Images; p. 22 NASA/NOAA; p. 26 Michael Blann/Digital Vision/ Thinkstock; p. 28 Andy Nelson/The Christian Science Monitor/Getty Images; p. 30 Miguel Navarro/Stone/Getty Images; p. 36 Ramin Talaie/Bloomberg/Getty Images; p. 41 Chip Somodevilla/Getty Images; p. 43 Lyhne/MCT/ Newscom; p. 46 iStockphoto/Thinkstock; p. 49 Universal Images Group/Getty Images; interior background (globe) © www.istockphoto.com/m-a-r-i; back cover (world), interior background chudo-yudo/Shutterstock.com.

Designer: Nicole Russo; Photo Researcher: Amy Feinberg